BETTINA

BETTINA

Guy Schoeller

THAMES AND HUDSON

Translated from the French by Francisca Garvie

First published in Great Britain in 1998
by Thames and Hudson Ltd, London

Copyright © 1998 Éditions Assouline, Paris
Translation copyright © 1998 Thames and Hudson Ltd, London

British Library Cataloguing-in-Publication Data

A catalogue record for this book is available from the British Library

ISBN 0-500-01894-4

Printed and bound in Italy

a t the age of eighteen a rather impecunious girl left her childhood home in Normandy to go to Paris. By the time she was twenty-five, she had changed her name and image; become famous and adulated; and featured on the cover of the world's leading magazines. At thirty, she fell in love and dropped everything, only to lose the man she loved five years later. Yet her enthusiasm for life remains triumphant − Bettina is still beautiful, strong, tender and courageous.

Born Simone Micheline Bodin, Bettina spent the early years of her life in the Elbeuf region of Normandy. Her father left the family home when she was six months old and she and her sister Catherine, who was three years older, were brought up by their warm and loving mother, who was a nursery-school teacher. Bettina's childhood was a happy one and, at the age of twelve, her mother encouraged her to learn to paint.

When war broke out, she and her sister were sent to stay with their grandmother in Angers. When their grandmother was killed in a bombing raid, the two girls moved to Agen before returning to

Elbeuf, where they lived until the Liberation four years later. Bettina emerged from these difficult years and from her several brushes with death unscathed and perhaps stronger, having learnt that she was naturally fearless. Her strength of character continued to grow and she proved to be an exceptionally well-balanced person. Her faith in life and her vitality were assets that encouraged her to take unusual decisions on her journey through life and Bettina loved living for the present too much to worry about her future.

Like all girls of her age, Bettina dreamed. But unlike most, she soon began to live out her dreams. Having seen Janine Charrat dancing *The Dying Swan* at the cinema one day, she immediately decided to become a dancer. She made herself a pair of ballet shoes by stuffing the toes of some espadrilles and began to learn to dance with a friend who was equally inexperienced but equally enthusiastic. A few months later they appeared on stage at a local youth club party. There Bettina caught the eye of an American dancer who gave her her first real ballet shoes and also taught her barre exercises and tap dancing. Bettina turned out to have superb deportment and an instinctive sense of pose.

At eighteen she needed to earn her own living. She decided to go and live in Paris, which was something she had longed to do ever since her sister Catherine, a dental technician, had moved there. Whenever Catherine returned to Elbeuf, she would be dressed in the latest Parisian fashions and her little sister was tremendously impressed by these outfits. Bettina saw them as the epitome of chic and loved trying on her sister's dresses, shoes and silk stockings. Deciding there was no future for her in Normandy, Bettina launched herself into the unknown with more ambition than resources. She travelled to Paris, intent on becoming a fashion designer.

to begin with, she lived with a family in Avenue de Villiers and looked after the children. Shortly afterwards, she managed to arrange an interview with Jacques Costet, a young couturier who had recently opened his showrooms at 4, Rue de la Paix. That interview was to change her life.

The young couturier, dressed with *élégance zazou* – a rather eccentric French fashion of the early 1940s – was in fact less interested in her designs than in the young woman herself. Costet ended the interview by asking Bettina to try on a magnificent dress. When she came out of the changing room, she found the assembled staff of the couture house waiting for her in the main salon – and that moment sealed her fate. She dazzled them all with her unaffected manner and natural poise. Costet surprised her by saying: 'Come back this afternoon. You will start as a model!' The second chapter of Bettina's life began as she embarked on an extraordinary and immensely successful twelve-year career.

On the afternoon of the interview with Costet, 1 June 1944, she herself did not model. Instead she watched the other models, observing the feverish haste with which they changed, hearing the nervous yelps when their skin caught in their zips, noting the speed with which they did their hair, skilfully draped their shawls and reached for their bags, umbrellas and other accessories.

The next day she modelled her first collection in front of an audience which was enthralled and delighted by her refreshing inexperience. Her pretty face and round cheeks, her freckles, her innate grace, everything about her conspired to captivate the clients.

She was now in a position to leave the Avenue de Villiers and abandon her babysitting duties, and she moved into a tiny flat on the Rue Raynouard with Tony, another of Costet's models. This was to be only a brief interlude on her road to independence and to finding a place of her own.

Her starting salary was low and so luxuries were out of the question. Lunching on a sandwich and dining on a cup of coffee, it was not difficult to keep her perfect figure. She did not know many people and could not afford the trip back to Elbeuf often. This was far from the high life she had imagined – no cinemas or theatres and few restaurants, but still her faith in the future remained indestructible.

The very first photographs of her date back to the Costet period, by which time she had already caught the eye of the Seeberger brothers, who introduced her to the world of the visual image.

a year later Bettina fell madly in love with a man named Benno Graziani and left Jacques Costet's couture house. She abandoned her career to be with Benno and they spent their first year together in Juan-les-Pins. Having returned to Paris in December 1946, where they got married, the former model decided to go back to work and made an appointment with Lucien Lelong. On the way to his office, she met a slightly chubby young man who approached her timidly, saying: 'If Monsieur Lelong does not employ you, I will, because I am about to open my own couture house.' It was Christian Dior! However, Lelong did take her on but she quickly became bored and left. Her next move was to Jacques Fath. When she turned up at his couture house, Fath welcomed her in his usual friendly fashion and took her on at once.

It was Fath who christened her Bettina. Their meeting marked the beginning of her metamorphosis and her life changed yet again. It was a happy time when everything she did was a success and her salary rocketed, increasing fivefold. The Fath couture house, in a magnificently furnished mansion on the Avenue Pierre-Ier-de-Serbie, was extremely friendly and welcoming and the models' changing room was one of the prettiest in Paris. Bettina made friends with Louise, Doudou, Tulipe and Renée, but it was Sophie, who was later to marry the producer Anatol Litvak, who became her best friend.

At that time, every couture house had to have its own models, who were attached to a particular couturier and presented and showed only his designs. As happened later when Givenchy and Audrey Hepburn teamed up together, the meeting between Bettina and Fath heralded the creation of a new style.

from the time Bettina first presented one of his collections, Jacques Fath created some thirty dresses for her. He was not particularly inspired by the 'New Look', so designed clothes with simple lines that only Bettina knew how to wear in such a way as to make them look both chic and natural. Fath created a genuine style for her, aimed mainly at the ordinary woman in the street. Indeed, at only 5' 5", Bettina was hardly the archetypal model. Her appeal was different – she was natural and fresh, graceful and lively. Her air of chic provided a refreshing contrast to the sophistication that made most of the models of that period look so frozen and stiff.

She became Fath's muse and quite often she was the one who suggested the ideas which he then elaborated. Fath presented Bettina everywhere as his star model, although fortunately the loathsome term 'top model' had not yet been coined. The public was charmed and the name Bettina came to stand for modernity and elegance.

Although she did not see herself as photogenic, her career really took off in front of the camera and soon all the fashion magazines wanted pictures of her. Jean Chevalier, one of the great photographers of the time, was also artistic director of the magazine *Elle*, created and edited by Hélène Lazareff. He introduced the two women and their meeting resulted in Bettina's first cover photo. The three of them got on well together and during that time Bettina featured on the most prominent pages of the magazine. Hélène Lazareff was *the* undisputed fashion guru of her time and her influence could make or break a career. She was particularly fond of Bettina and the young model became a regular guest at the sacrosanct Sunday lunches that Pierre and Hélène Lazareff gave in their house in Louveciennes, near Paris, to which all the famous names of the era were invited. It was a kind of consecration for Bettina, who was introduced to the most talented figures in politics, the arts, literature and, of course, fashion.

naturally gifted, indeed almost too gifted, Bettina had become the top cover girl in France within a matter of months. She captivated *Vogue*, which used her on their covers, and soon everyone who counted in the fashion press was after her − all, that is, except the American magazine *Harper's Bazaar*, since they were the legendary rivals of *Vogue*.

Little by little, she learnt to make use of her face and to employ all the secrets of make-up. She camouflaged her freckles with white foundation and hollowed out her cheeks by applying black shadow beneath her cheekbones. She emphasized her eyes with elegant black lines which made them appear both larger and brighter, and Irving Penn taught her how black lipstick could be used to create a contrast to the white of her face. She spent hours experimenting, transforming her appearance and creating a sophisticated image for herself, since models had to apply their own make-up and do their own hair for the photo shoots. Frequently they even used their own accessories to 'finish off' their outfits, but luckily it was the heyday of the hat, which solved a number of problems. The sittings were often a great strain and models had to learn how to wait and be prepared to produce the perfect image at a moment's notice. Fused lights, the heat of the projectors, creases in dresses were all familiar frustrations at these long posing sessions. But being a star model involved having to look divine even in the most uncomfortable positions, and here Bettina was unrivalled! Courage, good temper and hard work were all part of the 'Bettina' phenomenon.

Jacques Fath put the finishing touches on her new image by sending her to Georgel, the most highly reputed hairdressing salon of the time, and asking the master himself to cut her magnificent red mane. He had imported a new look from America and Bettina emerged from Georgel's salon almost shaven, with her hair cropped to within half an inch of her scalp. *Paris Match* immediately did a feature on the 'most photographed woman in France' and hundreds of admiring women hastened to copy her crew cut. Bettina had launched a new fashion and Fath created his famous series of rosebuttoned blouses especially for the occasion. Despite her dizzying success, she remained faithful to Fath for a long time.

She did a great many photo shoots and all the world's top fashion photographers fought over her, among them Irving Penn, Dick Dormer, Norman Parkinson, Erwin Blumenfeld, Henry Clarke, Gordon Parks and Jean-Philippe Charbonnier. Even Henri Cartier-

Bresson, who was normally so anti-fashion photography, was enthralled by her and photographed her in an informal setting, producing magnificent pictures. By the age of twenty-two, she had become the most famous model of her time.

a t the request of the great American photographer Irving Penn, for whom she had already posed in Paris, *Vogue* invited Bettina to the United States, where she joined the famous and recently opened Eileen Ford agency in June 1950. The life of a model in New York was quite different from that in Paris, where good humour always prevailed. Nothing was left to chance in America! The regime was one of strict discipline and everything was calculated, timed and checked at a time when modelling agencies did not yet exist in Paris.

But Bettina's private life was going downhill. Benno Graziani liked to party, go out on the town and see friends, but Bettina didn't have the energy to work all day and then socialize at night. They divorced and she moved to the Hôtel Montaigne, by the Bar des Théâtres. It was a lively, bustling area, the heart of artistic life in Paris, and only a stone's throw from the couture house of Fath, her friend, counsellor and confidant.

Bettina was single once again and adulated. Her next love, a thirty-five-year-old publisher, gave her a new outlook on Paris and introduced her to other publishers and writers: Gaston Gallimard became a true friend, followed by Louis Guilloux, William Faulkner, Joseph Kessel, Georges Simenon, Jean Genet and Jacques Prévert, who wrote a poem about her for a set of articles in the *Album du Figaro*.

She travelled widely. Her work took her to the United States, Brazil and Argentina and, with the help of her publisher friend, she discovered the joys of Italy. They went to Capri, where she met the Italian writer Curzio Malaparte, then to Naples, Rome and Florence. Guiding her in her reading and music, her new love introduced her to a life that she relished.

I n 1952 Bettina joined Hubert de Givenchy and helped him start his couture house. She thoroughly enjoyed working with Givenchy, who encouraged her to participate in all he did. She not only modelled, but also became involved in public relations and launched many of the famous couturier's creations. Everyone remembers the 'Bettina blouse' that she was shown wearing in every magazine and by all the leading photographers. But helping to start up a couture house demanded sacrifices and Bettina gave up posing for photo shoots for a while to devote herself entirely to the couturier, who was becoming increasingly successful. She accompanied him everywhere, which included a trip to New York, where she modelled his creations while also acting as his press attaché at the famous 'April in Paris' charity ball held in the Waldorf Astoria. There the television producer Edward R. Murrow offered her work and a film producer proposed a Hollywood contract, but the thought of being tied to a seven-year contract with a large studio did not tempt her. With no regrets, she chose independence instead and returned to Paris, where her publisher was waiting for her. He, however, was unpredictable, temperamental and a wanderer, and she left him. Her next love affair was with Peter Viertel, a Hollywood author and scriptwriter.

She discovered a new world, the world of the cinema, actors, directors and producers. Among those she met were Greta Garbo, Elizabeth Taylor, Gregory Peck, the Bogarts, Ava Gardner, John

Huston, Irving Shaw and Charlie Chaplin. Although she embraced a truly American lifestyle during her stays in Hollywood, she never stopped feeling nostalgic for Paris.

Her career peaked in 1955. Photographs of Bettina appeared in the press the world over and she worked flat out. The fees she charged for posing were enormous – seven thousand French francs an hour – and quite unprecedented at the time. She was sought after by everyone and was invited to appear at all major events – a rose was even named after her and Shell, the oil company, asked her to help launch its first computer, which was accessed by the password 'Bettina'.

It was during this period that Bettina met Prince Aly Khan, with whom she had already crossed paths in 1948 when she was modelling for Jacques Fath. She left the fashion world for the prince, abandoning all the couture houses overnight, and gave up posing for magazines. Five years later she faced yet another upheaval in her life when she lost the man who was going to marry her. He died in a car accident, with her at his side.

●

In spite of her premature departure from the fashion world and the abrupt end to her spectacular modelling career, Bettina has remained a leading figure in the field. The proof lies in the many photographs of her – it is not always easy to distinguish the private snap from the posed magazine image – and in her frequent reappearances in a world that has never forgotten her. She was the source of inspiration behind an entire collection which Coco Chanel asked her to pose for and present in 1969 and Emanuel Ungaro then asked her to model a collection for him. And fashion magazines, intrigued by this famous silhouette that no

14

longer appears in public, have never lost interest in her. Bettina loves fashion; she has played with it, used it, followed it and led it, and has always delighted in immersing herself in the field. Instinctively recognizing the talent of a couturier before the rest of the world and equally at ease wearing Balenciaga, Chanel and Yves Saint Laurent, she has chosen Azzedine Alaïa, one of the rare undisputed creative talents of our times, to dress her, and she has now worn Alaïa's creations for several years. The passage of time has done nothing to quench Bettina's keen eye for the world of fashion, which she continues to survey with interest, good humour and curiosity.

Bettina was the greatest French model of her time and one of its brightest ever stars. She reigned over the difficult, nascent world of the photographic image, created her own style and has left an indelible mark on the history of fashion. And yet she has managed to remain herself – genuine, strong and simply divine. Bettina symbolizes both naturalness and style.

Bettina will always be Bettina.

4669

4666

4670

4667

4671

4668

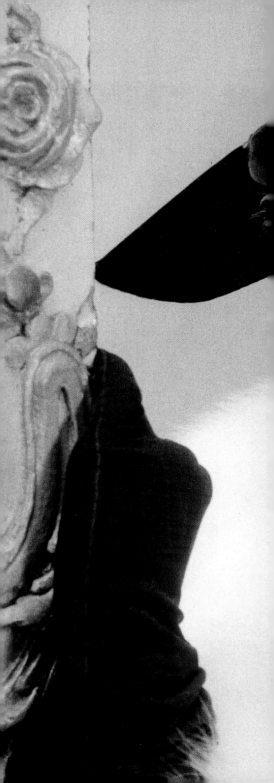

22 December, 1951

PICTURE POST

BRITAIN'S NATIONAL WEEKLY

22 DECEMBER 1951

OVERSEAS EDITION

				INTERNATIONAL SELLING PRICES			
ARGENTINA	75 CENTAVOS	FINLAND	35 FINMARKS	NETHERLANDS	50 CENTS		
AUSTRIA	3 SCHILLINGS	FRANCE	50 FRANCS	NORWAY	1 KRONE		
BELGIUM	7 FRANCS	GERMANY	60 PFENNIG	PAKISTAN	8 ANNAS		
BRITISH WEST INDIES	1 SHILLING	GIBRALTAR	1 SHILLING	PORTUGAL	4.50 ESCUDOS		
BURMA	11 ANNAS	INDIA	11 ANNAS	SWEDEN	90 ÖRE		
CANADA	15 CENTS	ISRAEL	50 PRUTTOT	SWITZERLAND	70 CENTIMES		
CEYLON	70 CENTS	ITALY	100 LIRE	UNITED STATES OF			
DENMARK	1 KRONE	MALAYA	45 CENTS	AMERICA	15 CENTS		
EGYPT	5 PIASTRES	MALTA	1 SHILLING	WEST & EAST AFRICA	1 SHILLING		

PRICE IN AUSTRALIA, NEW
ZEALAND, SOUTH AFRICA
AND RHODESIA

1/-

BY SPECIAL ARRANGEMENT PRICE TO H.M. FORCES . . 6 PENCE

VOL. 53 • NO. 12

Quick

Modebericht aus Paris:
Diors kurzer Rock

NR. 36 JAHRGANG 6 MÜNCHEN, 6. SEPTEMBER 1953 50 PF

Belgien: bfrs. 7, Dänemark: dkr. 1.—, England: sh. 1.—, Frankreich: ffrs. 55, Holland: 60, ...chen: 1.100,
...burg: bfrs 7, Norwegen: nkr. 1.—, Österreich: S 3.50, Saarland: Frs. 50, Schweden: ...

VOGUE "ARRANGÉ" PAR PICASSO

Elegante Welt

ELLE

...nte :
...ollections

...méro
...bum

ALBUM
FIGARO

PRIX 500 fr.

10 ans de moins
Les nouvelles co
Mystères
et
Mirages des r
Les cadeaux qui co

PARIS
MATCH
N° 56   19 AVRIL 1950   50 fr.

Dans ce numéro :

LE TESTAMENT
DE
BOGOMOLETZ

U. S. News révèle :

LA VÉRITÉ
SUR LES
SOUCOUPES
VOLANTES

Le document
intégral

Et la suite
du reportage
qui passionne
l'Angleterre :

ELIZABETH
femme inconnue

ADAME

Herbst- und Wintermode

ELLE

La Française
sait-elle
s'habiller ?

ALPAGA ?
PRINCE
DE GALLES ?
TWEED ?

Chronology

1944 Bettina arrives in Paris, after the Liberation, hoping for a career as a fashion designer. She has an interview with a young couturier, Jacques Costet, who takes her on as a model.
First photo shoots with the Seeberger brothers.

1945 Bettina leaves for Juan-les-Pins with Benno Graziani and gives up modelling.

1946 Bettina marries Benno Graziani in Paris, divorcing him a few years later. She returns to the world of fashion, working first with Lucien Lelong and then with Jacques Fath.
Her career as a photographic model takes off. She meets Hélène Lazareff and Jean Chevalier, known as Cheval, and they begin working together.

1950 Bettina leaves Jacques Fath's to concentrate solely on her photographic modelling career.
She goes to the United States, where she works for the Eileen Ford agency in New York.

1952 Bettina joins Hubert de Givenchy and helps him launch his couture house.

1954 While continuing to model for Givenchy and to pose for photographs, she creates the first knitwear collections for a new designer in Monaco, Jacques Heim.

1955 Bettina's career reaches its peak.
She meets Prince Aly Khan and abandons her career for love.

1969 Coco Chanel creates a collection inspired by Bettina.

1972 Bettina becomes couture director for Emanuel Ungaro.
Françoise Sagan writes an article about the red-headed Bettina entitled 'L'Eminence rousse' for French *Vogue*.

1974 Bettina is put in charge of public relations for Valentino in Paris.

1978 Bettina reasserts her independence. She travels widely, especially in Africa and Latin America; her accounts of her trips are published in American *Vogue* and in *Elle*.

1990 'Bettina' exhibition is held in the Galerie Jean-Gabriel Mitterand in Paris, during the 'Mois de la photo' (photography month), in which Thomas Gunther participates. Frédéric Mitterand dedicates a programme to Bettina, which also features all the major photographers as well as Lauren Bacall, Jeanne Moreau, Azzedine Alaïa, Helmut Berger and Françoise Sagan, among others.

Hat in black velvet and striped raw silk with a sealskin coat by Renel. The 'Infante' line leaves the brow bare and softens the line of the neck, creating an asymmetrical effect that is echoed in the coat. Photo by Henry Clarke, published in French Vogue, *September 1953. © ADAGP, 1998.*

Bettina

Bettina aged four. 'I was so scared of the camera that when my mother let go of my hand and told me not to move, I didn't dare move a finger! It may be the height of narcissism, but if I'd had a girl, I would have liked her to resemble that child!' © All rights reserved. **'Bringing an evening dress to life in front of the lens** was great fun, especially dresses made of raw silk – their weight, the fall of the material and the rustling noise they make are so sensual.' Dress by Jacques Fath (c. 1950). © All rights reserved.

One of the early photos of Bettina as a model, posing for Jacques Costet in front of the Relais Plazza, Avenue Montaigne, in Paris. Photo by Seeberger (c. 1948). © All rights reserved. **The Bettina look.** Photo taken on the Place de la Concorde, Paris, before it was opened to traffic, by Arik Népik for French *Vogue*, September 1951. © All rights reserved.

Bettina's animated and unaffected style captivated the world's photographers. 'In a summer dress, outside, in mid-winter… and she's still smiling!' © All rights reserved. **With Jacques Fath, who launched her.** From left to right are Jacques Fath, Bettina, Sophie and Doudou. Photo taken during a trip to the South of France to present a Fath collection (c. 1952). © All rights reserved.

'You often had to play games with the camera. Here I am holding a "Dear John" letter! For every shot we had to create a scenario, thought up by either the photographer or myself.' Photo by Potier. © All rights reserved. **The early days of sportswear** with this sage-green twin-set, designed by Givenchy for the boutique selling his designs in Parc Monceau, where the photograph was taken. 'Later, I created my own knitwear collection for Heim.' © All rights reserved.

'With neither hairdressers nor make-up artists to help models at the time this photo was taken, it was lucky that hats were in fashion!' Photo by Henry Clarke. © ADAGP, 1998.

Wearing a dress by Jacques Fath (Autumn 1947) with romantic pearls and white satin gloves trimmed with white fox (1947). 'I did my own hair for the catwalks (every afternoon at three o'clock). Here it looks so romantic!' Photo by Harry Meerson. © All rights reserved. **'Paris was the ideal backdrop** for fashion photographs.' Afternoon suit (Autumn 1951). Photo by Russel, published in the *Album du Figaro*, September–October 1951. © *Marie Claire.*

76

'You needed a perfect figure to wear jersey. The photographer and I would look for the best way to express the line of the dress.' (c. 1948). © All rights reserved. 'I still have a penchant for hats ever since that time. As for veils, they were so feminine that they immediately dictated one's whole attitude. Hats were an integral part of the ensemble that was shown to the clients, since we had to be elegant from head to toe.' © All rights reserved.

Fath dresses (Spring 1951), with Bettina on the right. 'The theme of this photo was the bustiers made of flowers. The full skirts accentuated our narrow waists.' © All rights reserved.

Portrait of Bettina by Irving Penn, after a modelling session. 'I was about to leave but still had my make-up on when Irving Penn suggested this portrait. I am wearing my American jacket that I wore for years over a man's shirt. It was my favourite outfit.' Bettina Collection. 'Irving Penn taught me a great deal. He wanted make-up to provide strong contrasts, so here I'm wearing black lipstick.' Photos by Irving Penn, Paris 1950. Courtesy of *Vogue*. © 1950 (renewed 1978 by Condé Nast Publications).

'A 1950s Watteau: *L'Indifférent* was to be reborn for an evening, dressed by Jacques Fath in a white satin battle-dress.' (Winter 1949). Photograph taken in Nadar's studio and published in the *Album du Figaro*, No. 22, February–March 1950. Photo by Henry Clarke. Bettina Collection. © ADAGP, 1998. The same jacket in pearl-grey satin photographed in a more casual and relaxed pose. Black velvet skirt and hat.' © All rights reserved.

Bettina, dressed by Robert Piguet and photographed by Irving Penn. 'Penn's photos always required a lot of strength in the pose.' Photo published in American *Vogue*, 1 September 1950. Courtesy of *Vogue*. © 1950 (renewed 1978 by Condé Nast Publications). 'Posing in a sheath evening dress, with short hair, was revolutionary at that time.' © All rights reserved.

Copacabana Palace Hotel, Rio de Janeiro. Photo taken by the pool as the models prepare to present a Dior collection. Carlos, 'a friend and admirer', is holding a mirror for Bettina. Sophie Litvak is in the background. Photo by Jean Manzon. © All rights reserved. Bettina wearing a Dior outfit from the 'Diabolo' line. Photo by Irving Penn, published in American *Vogue*, 1 September 1950. Courtesy of *Vogue*. © 1950 (renewed 1978 by Condé Nast Publications).

Cover girl of the international press during the 1950s. On the right, Bettina is wearing a Dior dress and the photographer Robert Randall is in the background. 'It was Robert's assistant who had the idea for this photo.' © All rights reserved.

Wearing an embroidered hat by Rébé, 1953. 'I loved making the fur fall backwards off my shoulder to give it more life and to inspire the photographer. It was the same with the pearls.' Photo by Henry Clarke. Bettina Collection. © ADAGP, 1998. '**Photo session for Korrigan sweaters.** I posed for the entire catalogue – each photo showed a new sweater in a new scenario.' Photo by Kublin. © Kublin.

In her little rented studio on the Avenue Montaigne in Paris. '*Life* magazine did a whole feature on me, which involved photographing me at home. Here I am shown with my cat Agathe.' Photo from an article published in *Life* magazine. © All rights reserved. '**Red Shoes' dress by Jacques Fath** (Autumn 1950). 'After this, large theatrical stoles were often used.' Photo by Irving Penn, published in American *Vogue*, 1 September 1950. Courtesy of *Vogue*. © 1950 (renewed 1978 by Condé Nast Publications).

'**Gloves were an essential accessory** for sittings. They "finished off" an outfit and often inspired the pose.' © All rights reserved. '**I love the look** of this severe Christian Dior suit.' Make-up by Bettina. © All rights reserved.

Between two photo sessions in Rio de Janeiro, Bettina still found time to pose for the photographer Jean Manzon, wearing her own clothes. © All rights reserved. **Bettina poses in an embroidered dress by Lempereur.** 'This photo reflects all the elegance and freshness of Paris in the 1950s.' Photo by Lionel Kazan, published in *Elle*, No. 494, 30 May 1955. © *Elle*/Scoop.

Givenchy dress in jersey wool, 1952. 'I posed for Givenchy and also looked after public relations for him.' Photo by Maurice Tabard, published in the *Album du Figaro*, No. 39, December 1952. Bettina Collection. © All rights reserved. '**Gloves, hat, veil** – it was that era. I liked posing, it was both instinctive and enjoyable.' © All rights reserved.

Behind the scenes. Hélène Lazareff is working on the framing of a photo with Jean Chevalier, photographer and art director of *Elle*. Photo by N.R. Farban for *Life* magazine. © All rights reserved. **The result as seen by Elle readers.** This photo by Jean Chevalier, showing Bettina wearing a shirt from Hubert de Givenchy's first collection, christened the 'Bettina blouse', was shown all round the world. © *Elle*/Scoop.

Bettina wearing a brown jersey two-piece. 'Like stretch fabric, ribbed jersey created a very body-hugging line.' © All rights reserved. **Photo shoot on the River Seine,** in the early 1950s. 'I am wearing my own sandals, made in Capri. Models were often asked to bring their own accessories to "finish off" an outfit. These are still very fashionable.' © All rights reserved.

In the international press, a cover wasn't a cover without Bettina. © All rights reserved.

Astrakhan jacket by Revillon, 1952. 'Same clothes, same place, but different pose and look.' Photos by Emile Savitry. © Rapho.

'**Henry Clarke, with whom I often worked,** became a close friend. We were both very pleased with the modern look of this white wool coat by Jacques Fath.' (Spring 1951). Photo by Henry Clarke. © ADAGP, 1998. **'Playing the extreme sophisticate** was great fun.' Jacques Fath (Spring 1951). © All rights reserved.

Bettina, wearing her own clothes, posing for the photographer Roger Prigent, during a trip to the United States. © All rights reserved. **Waiting in the wings** before presenting the Hubert de Givenchy collection, for the 'April in Paris' charity ball. Dress-shirt cape over an evening gown. 'This gown was highly successful and was greeted with much applause.' Photo by Milton Greene. © All rights reserved.

Bettina launches the crew cut, inspired by the American marines. Jacques Fath had brought this idea back from one of his trips to the United States. © All rights reserved. **Shocking pink jersey wool sweater,** created by Maxime de La Falaise for an English knitwear company. Photo taken in London in 1954. Bettina wore this sweater for many years. Bettina Collection. © All rights reserved.

'**I often wore my own clothes** for hat photos.' © All rights reserved. **Tweed hat, raincoat and gum boots** formed part of Bettina's wardrobe. Photo taken at the start of a fox hunt near Dublin, Ireland, in 1953. 'Following the hunt on foot or by car is a sport in itself. I kept this hat for years.' Bettina Collection. © All rights reserved.

Private life. Sable-coloured Dior ensemble, worn at the races at Longchamp in 1958. Photo by Patrice Habans. © *Elle*/Scoop. **In front of the camera.** Couture sportswear by Jacques Fath – linen jacket and striped trousers, photographed by Carter (Summer 1954). © All rights reserved.

In 1990, Pierre & Gilles asked Bettina to pose for them. They turned her into a schoolgirl saint for their exhibition of saints. © Pierre & Gilles. '**I often presented hat collections** on the catwalk. I had my own outfit for these shows – a black jersey sweater with a high roll-neck, tight black trousers and ballet shoes or pumps, like a cat burglar. The effect highlighted the hat.' © All rights reserved.

A shoot organized by Mario Testino at Azzedine Alaïa's, 1992. 'Azzedine is certainly one of the most talented couturiers I have ever met and Mario Testino is one of the great fashion photographers of the 1990s.' **Skirt and bolero in a straw-based fabric by Alaïa.** Courtesy of Mario Testino. Photo taken at a shoot organized by German *Vogue* in 1996 during a joint interview with Bettina and René Gruau, the famous fashion designer. © Condé Nast Publications.

The author and publishers wish to thank Bettina for her assistance in producing this volume.

They also thank Pierre & Gilles, Mario Testino, Valérie Guillaume, curator in charge of twentieth-century fashion at the Musée de la Mode de la Ville de Paris, the Musée Galliera, Sylvie Richoux (Musée de la Mode et du Textile) and Thomas Gunther.

Finally, our thanks go to Nicole Chamson and Chantal Bermude (ADAGP, Paris), Claudine Legros (*Elle*/Scoop), Lorraine Mead (Condé Nast Publications, New York), Gwénaelle Dautricourt (*Marie Claire* Copyright) and Martine Tonon (Rapho).